CLIMATE CHANGED

The earth is a star.

We're already dead.

DUY

ĐOÀN

ALICE JAMES BOOKS
New Gloucester, ME
alicejamesbooks.org

ZOMBIE

VOMIT

MAD

LIBS

Alice James Books are published by Alice James Poetry Cooperative, Inc.

Alice James Books
Auburn Hall
60 Pineland Drive, Suite 206
New Gloucester, ME 04260
www.alicejamesbooks.org

Names: Đoàn, Duy, author.
Title: Zombie vomit mad libs / Duy Đoàn.
Description: New Gloucester, Maine : Alice James Books, 2024.
Identifiers: LCCN 2024028924 (print) | LCCN 2024028925 (ebook)
    ISBN 9781949944686 (trade paperback) | ISBN 9781949944402 (epub)
Subjects: LCGFT: Poetry.
Classification: LCC PS3604.O17 Z36 2024 (print) | LCC PS3604.O17 (ebook)
    DDC 811/.6--dc23/eng/20240624
LC record available at https://lccn.loc.gov/2024028924
LC ebook record available at https://lccn.loc.gov/2024028925

Alice James Books gratefully acknowledges support from individual donors, private
foundations, the National Endowment for the Arts, and the Poetry Foundation
(https://www.poetryfoundation.org).

Cover photo: *risk assessment (fugue state / : h** volant touch.)*, 2020–2021, by Catalina Ouyang

CONTENTS

ZOMBIE VOMIT MAD LIBS

CONTAGION

Say something about wake and dream. The tranquil side of happiness where one of us promised the other we'd be. Vermeer's earring reminds you of Leonardo's ermine. Leonardo's ermine reminds me of Vermeer's earring. Two silky-ermine-studded ears. *If you are a pet or horse owner, please press 1.* You touched something that was moving, and now everything is watermarked. Every sheet of paper, every PDF, every page. The guinea pig, a stethoscope, the bass. Would you rather ride a horse or a donkey. The horse is smaller than the donkey, but I won't tell you how big the donkey is. Both eat leaves; one eats only dead ones, the other only green. I won't say which which. The horse's name is Donkey. The donkey's name is Horse. Wait a minute. . .   We were leading a horse to water.

ZOMBIE

One had this problem where   they were always looking for the radius of things.

OXYTOCIN

A good way to change your
name is to get a divorce.
There was that one time
she drew the dog's shadow.
There was that other time she
melted the painting's face off.
A shark swam between my
legs during freeze tag, and
we had to free her until
she caught the last-one-
standing. She caught him by
the torso.

          The only time
I ever saw the two of them
flirt, she asked him, *What's
your favorite Day of the Dead
memory.*
          I don't have one.

What's your favorite emoji.

The one with the face. *No,
I mean,*
          out of all of them.

The one with the face.

FLEAS,

Stop pooping on my son.

Stop pooping on my daughter.

    I   will fṳck you ụp.

I will jȧb
my iPhone

at your little orbital bones.

It's an iPhone SỀ.

It's from 1973.

for my mèos
Nghiệp and MâyMây

iPhone VC

Small, sleek,   hard to
type on.

Impóssible to detect   when
it's in your pockêt.

The only thing,

one GI says,

worth shooting at.

—

Nòw

whất did they shoot at

when they rotated

bạck

into their own violent
wôrld.

ZOMBIE

The crossing over was slow.

She couldn't remember. She couldn't
forget.

POET SUICIDES,
THIRTEEN-PENTAMETER SONNET

Humberto, René, Sophie, Sylvia.
Michel, Antonia, José María.

Arturo, Richard, John and Konstantin.

Jane, Rachel, John, Amelia. Danielle,
Karin, Dolores,
              Sara, May and Jan.

Jean-Joseph, Yun,
              Marina and Teresa.

Yukio Lucan Nika Allen Jaime Qu.
Eli Liam Charlotte Sara Lu.

And Joe and Paul.
              Pierre, María.
And Jacques, and Jacques, and
Jacques and Anna.

And Arthur and Hart and Thomas and Chen.
And Sergei and Deborah and Yulia

and Jens. And Georg
              and Rozz
and Zhao

and
Anne.

MAD LIB WITH ANNE SEXTON

Most eye floaters are caused

by age-related

garages that occur as

the vodka-like substance

(vitreous) inside your eyes

becomes more liquid.

Microscopic gemstone jewelry

outside the car

tend to clump

and can cast tiny fur coats on

your retina. The fur coats you see

are called floaters.

SONNET WITH POETS IN IT

_____ committed suicide in the following years:

1929, 1935, 1974, 1963.
1964, 1938, 1969.

1912, 1984, 1972, 1951,

1982, 2009, 1950, 1996. 1978,
1941, 1857,
          1984, 1996, 1956.

1937, 2003,
          1941, 1921.

1970, 65 CE, 2002, 1926, 1974, 278 BCE.
1978, 2007, 1928, 1933, c. 684 or 686.

1990, 1970.
          1945, 2003.
1923, 1929,
1919, 1947.

1945, 1932, 1770, 1966.
1925, 2009, 1991,

1976. 1914,
          1998,
1367,

and
Anne

and
and

A LITTLE BIT DOPAMINE,
A LITTLE BIT CONVERSATION

"Íven the teensiest of curtsies
will make your shadow go away.

If you envision tucking your chin
down, but actually don't, the door
will swell beyond the height
of its frame

even when you're telling it
not to do so, and
even if you rebuke it
for paralyzing you while
you sleep—"

I think I may have
heard someone argue this
unsuccessfully once, though
I don't know how come.

-

My body wants to find stasis.
But it only wants to remember
that it should want to when some
other body reminds it to

be sô.

Everyone here could be an
addict of the injectables
industry if they wanted to be.

-

Even the sunshine, when it goes,
it goes hand in hand with you.
Everyone here says this múnshine

tastes like moonshine if moonshine
had cough syrup in it. And that's
what I think, too. You're like a vine,
you keep repeating.

-

Best of luck!
Yours,
Duy Doan

Best of luck!
Yours,
Duy Doan

Best of luck!
Yours,
Duy Doan

Best of luck!
Yours,
Duy Doan

2046 IS ON THE 24TH FLOOR

Leslie Cheung was 11 years older than me when he committed suicide. April 1, which is my birthday.

The cabinet work of the Spruce Goose,
relentless with its evidence of mastery: birch precision and an
                                             obsession with cleanliness.

That stupid plane got off the ground for only 26 seconds, a triumph of prodigiousness and profligacy. In my third favorite movie with Leslie Cheung in it *Days of Being Wild,*   there's this really maudlin, overly-poetic metaphor

about a bird without legs that could never land.
It's the kind of metaphor you accept when you're taking in opera.
Every human-emotion spectacle
is scaled way up and dazzles.

The bird metaphor is kind of beautiful, though, I have to admit. And maybe it's even more beautiful not in English.   But what if Wong Kar-wai avoided using the

negative—   he could have avoided giving so much finality that Leslie's portrait became sentimental.

What if he just said the bird waited forever to alight.

In my least favorite of the trilogy   2046,   Tony Leung,
who also plays Leslie's lover in *Happy Together,*

says that Carina Lau (Lulu),

another victim to Leslie's fuckboy fuckery,   compared Leslie
                                                   with a bird that could never land.

            The bird metaphor   returning 14 years later.   The immense
tardiness of the Spruce Goose.

        But if Wong Kar-wai did follow my
suggestion for the metaphor,

and Tony Leung actually tells us,
                                She compared him to a bird
                                that waited forever to alight,
it wouldn't be fitting for Lulu to play the leading lady anymore.

And that's not what the audience wants
and needs.   *. . . always the leading lady,* Tony Leung says. A cigarette plays
                                                Perfidia in her gloved hand.

        In this world there are way more Tony Leung characters
                                than there are Leslie Cheung characters.
You'd be taking a dishonest position if you didn't admit there are way fewer Leslies.
    It's just that he goes around hurting a lot of Tonies. Even
    when he's only setting out to hurt himself.
                                There's the famous scene in *Happy*

when he's slow-dancing with Tony,   their love   becomes a sway in a forever,
                                and then there's the scene in *Days*

when he's dancing   to mambo   by himself in   the mirror.

ZOMBIE BABIES

(love letter,
                    one baby to another):

hot damn

ur not fucking around

u really know how to see things
thru

LET THE RIGHT ONE IN —
FIRST MEETING SCENE (IN REWIND)

Exterior – Apartment Building – Night
A BOY, twelve, stands with a TREE to his right.

Boy:
friend? your be to want I sure so you Are

The boy, left.
Across from him, a GIRL VAMPIRE, twelve, stands with a JUNGLE GYM behind
her. She turns around and walks towards him, stops halfway.

Girl Vampire:
is. it way the just That's
reason? a be to have there Does

Boy:
mean? you do What

Girl Vampire:
friend. your be can't I know, you so Just

She walks backwards away from him, then, still facing him, floats onto the top of
the jungle gym.

Boy:
live? I where know you do How

She stops pointing at the window.

Girl Vampire:
you. to door Next

Boy:
live? you do where Seriously,

17

Girl Vampire:
gym. jungle the in here, right live I
Yeah. . .

Boy:
here? live you Do

Girl Vampire:
Nothing.

Boy:
doing? you are What
Nothing.

Girl Vampire:
doing? you are What

He turns to the tree and starts stabbing it.

ZOMBIE BABIES

(love letter,
           the other baby to the first
baby):

I like that you use the
infinitive

that way we don't have to worry
about their conjugations
when you're an outcast you can
only really trust the other
outcasts

"TALE OF THE TAPE"

Let the Right One In

is a love story. A horror vampire love story
with 0 sessions in front of a mirror, with 0
stakes through any hearts.

Oskar, 12,
has skin whiter
than the snow in Sweden. Eli, also 12,
has bad hygiene, especially if she hasn't eaten

for a long time.

—

In the opening credits, snow falls against a black
sky, and for some brief moments,
I feel like there's no audio
and we see nothing
of the city. Just snow and black.

Someday I'll ask a filmmaker about camera angles.

—

The movie is set
in Blackeberg,
a suburb of Stockholm,
in the 1980s.

Eli's hair is black.
Oskar's is blond.
They're about the same height—
typical height probably for twelve-year-olds.

—

There are 13
scenes with the both
of them in it. In their third-to-last
scene together, after 5
people have already died

because of her, Eli tells Oskar she has to go away. 2

minutes and 36 seconds later/19 shots

after, we see Oscar cry for the only
time in the movie—through
his window, snot hanging over his upper lip.
Tears.

—

Second scene with Eli and Oskar together: on the jungle gym
with a Rubik's Cube. Third
scene with them together: Rubik's Cube returned
fully solved. Fourth scene: *Oskar, you have to hit back.*
She's referring to his bullies. He teaches her Morse code—
*short long long short
long*

Fifth:

through the wall at night— S... W... E... E... T...
D...
R...
Eli is good at trees,
aging, falling, climbing hospitals,
mauling, losing weight,

—

not knowing her birth date,
solving problems,

protecting.

—

Even when the 3 bullies cut
his left cheek
open
with a switch,
Oskar doesn't cry.
Or when his mom rushes
him through the doorway, her right
hand gesturing violently. He doesn't cry

when his dad stops paying
attention to him and gets drunk,
sinking into depression
one shot of clear liquor at a time.

Or when the oldest bully
tries to hold him under water for 3 minutes.

One full round.

—

The first
time I saw the movie, I thought there were 3
artists who played Eli, but actually there are only 2.
And another plays
Eli's voice.

—

First
date scene / 2,412 seconds
in. Oskar shares candy with Eli, and she vomits
and makes a big hug
happen. *Oskar, do you like me?* Yeah, a lot.

If I wasn't a girl. . . would you still
like me?

—

Eli's love
poem to Oskar is written on the inside
of a tiny box.

Oskar's love poem is the Rubik's Cube when he
asks if she wants to keep it.

—

The second note we see
from Eli says: "Yours, . . ." The older
Eli's only lines are "Go!"

and "Please."

Håkan's final word is "Eli." Oskar has 3 main weapons.

—

Before I could picture
it in reverse, I watched the first meeting
scene at least 2 dozen times.

—

In the scene immediately after the last
time we see Oskar and Eli together,
he disappears into his bedroom and closes
the door behind him.
His mother beats on it.

In the next shot,

we see him in his room blocking
the door with a cane. We see 5 ½
toy cars—black, black,
blue, blue,

blue,
yel—

and he closes a door, door, trunk,
door, hood.

—

In the final scene where they're together,

they're on a train.

It's daytime.

Eli is in a cardboard box. She spells out
kiss.

Oskar is sitting at the window. He spells out

small kiss.

On the seat across from them is a red bag.

—

Before Eli goes through
Oskar's window, in the scene after Håkan willingly gives up
his blood

to her, she asks Oskar if she can enter.

—

Eli.

Want to go steady?

They're in bed; she's big

spoon. She sits up, and her eyes flutter. Her lips—
dried blood all over.

Oskar. . .

—

I'm not a girl.

—

Oh. . .

But do you want to go steady. . .

—

Let the
Right One In

premiered in a January. It was released
in Sweden that same October. It was directed

by Tomas Alfredson.

The film has 8 violent
scenes in it, __ shots

in the penultimate montage.
I'd say there are 3
main characters. 11 main events.
275
to 325 names of people in the end credits. 7 fighters.
2 love stories. 3
people in love. 2

with one another.

—

2008 • R • 1h 54min

ZZZZZ ZOMBIES

The thing is

they were all wearing masks   when they were asleep   .

EVERYTHING MEANS NOTHING COMPARES

Ants shouldn't do
burpees because
they would
burp themselves

into oblivion.
1 burpee can burn .16
calories, which
is nothing.

You were thinking
of a number
between 1
and 1 over
17 because
"Everything" means
that nothing is
special now.

How do you end
your most skillful, most
rapturous piece
of craft,

with a double
rainbow. What a
prompt that
would be.

Prompt:
Why would
anyone make
fun of the
double rainbow guy.

Clearly, he was just
overwhelmed by
something
transformative

and beautiful—
Maybe nothing
before was as
beautiful as

what he saw that day;
and what if, for the
rest of his life, he never
encounters anything

that moves him
as much as
that rainbow did. I *have*
YouTube-asked him:
Was it irreparable. Do
you feel a permanent
sense of loss.
Was it

shrooms. Was it Edith
Wharton's *Age of Innocence*
before the greatest
breakup you ever had.

I had a moment
like his once, before
YouTube—
bagpipes

being a kind of throat
singing. People's
pretentious metaphors
might be genuine

during heartache:
Are balancing acts
most interesting
when they almost fail

to be deceptive.
Are the wise things
wise people aphorize
to us wise. Maybe

it's our denominator
that's weak,
not my numerator.
Elliott Smith's

"Everything Means
Nothing to Me"
is a song about
a songbird that
waited till it was
thirty-four
to alight.
*People have died from
time to time, and*

*worms have
eaten them,
but not for love.*
We'd do well

to remember it's not
actually Shakespeare
who's saying this,
but Rosalind,

and it's possible
we're to understand
that she's wrong. It's

like how, on some
level, Prince's "Nothing
Compares 2 U"
can make you
wonder:

Did I escape that kind of
love, or am I in a constant
state of wanting
that kind of love.

A GIRL WALKS HOME ALONE AT NIGHT — FIRST KISS SCENE

Interior – Black and white. The VAMPIRE's bedroom – Night

POSTERS cover the walls: Michael Jackson Thriller *cover, Madonna* Madonna *cover, lots of other posters. There's a BED in the background, a DISCO BALL hanging from the middle of the room, a RECORD PLAYER against the right wall. It's Halloween.*

ARASH, dressed as a vampire, is lying face-up on the vampire's bed. He's on the comedown from E. The vampire is facing away from him, standing in front of the record player. She puts a record on. He's lying still. She starts the record…

0:14 – "Death" by White Lies is the song.

0:37 – Arash stirs.

0:48 – Lyrics start / "I love the feeling when we"

0:50 – "lift off."

>   *Four seconds after "lift off," but not AT "lift off"…*

0:54 – Arash sits straight up. He starts to stand, walks slowly towards the disco ball. We see that he is wearing a cape.

1:06 – He stands still below/in front of the ball, looking up at it.

>   *Ecstasy turns us into moths.*

1:12 – Slightly after "my window," he spins the ball.

DOPAMINE

The person I've been talking to
this last half year
recently upped their flirting game,
and my mind is kind of blown. Two logistics texts

and then a nurturing one. Two short answers and
then flirtatious. Five days. A few seconds.

And all the time
little charming deep weird ones:

eww the human body is filled
with countless holes $0
premium $0 copays $0
deductible

<3 ilysm

-

No contracts. No hidden
fees. No crodot card$.

Ily2

The lást time we'll ever have dinner together in a
restaurant with more than 25% capacity, two
mice scurried along the matte baseboard, wearing
coats, a tie, and heels.

We'll never see anything like that again.

Sőmething about two mammals in a
hefty kind of flight. Something about
Blue Planet's most successful mammals.

A GIRL WALKS HOME ALONE AT NIGHT — FIRST KISS SCENE

1:20 – CLOSER UP. The vampire on the right edge of frame. We see her from the shoulder up. Disco-ball-spinning-glitter in the background. Will-o'-the-wisp lights whipping across the posters over and over again. We watch her breathing. Slow, shallow breaths at regular intervals.

> *26 seconds. Our only purpose is to watch her breathe.*

The disco ball lights slow down but then start to quicken—they go from gliding slowly, smoothly across the posters to whipping across them again.

> *But there's no shadow passing through. Did the ball start up again by itself.*

1:46 – "fear's got a hold on me" / Arash enters the shot. The vampire is still facing the wall. Arash closes the distance slowly.

***

2:02 – He's halfway across the screen. We can see that he's predator but don't know if she's prey. / Music for verse 2 begins.

***

2:17 – "I love the quiet of the nighttime" / He's directly behind her. They are two parallel profiles. His nose and forehead touch her hair, just barely. Now her deepest breath, just slightly more perceptible than the ones before.

More breathing. Vampires do breathe. The film is much breathing.

2:31 – "I can feel my heart beating" / She starts to turn.

The longer the vampire takes to turn around,

the more time spring has to send the birds away. They come back

with new songs.

2:45 – The bassline, which went away some time ago, returns. / The vampire is still turning.

It looks like she could be standing on a little

tiny lazy Susan, someone's steady hand spinning her around slowly.

3:05 – She's still turning.

ZOMBIES AT A CROSS SIGNAL

...

lollipop. Yet in my heart I am go children slow.

—Anne _____

OXYTOCIN — SIBLINGS

For years after mom died, I
would get home late at
night and say, *Hi pop, where's
ma.*

    And he'd stay quiet, and
you'd chime up, *In bed.*

And I'd say, *Oh,
asleep (already).*

               Sometimes
he'd be drinking a highball and
watching the History
Channel. Sometimes at
Christmas, it was whiskey in
his Santana shirt. We kept
this joke up a minute.

KISSING SANTA

Praise Yahweh and His Son you
saw mommy kissing Santa Claus
last night. She deserves to be happy.
She's the one to teach us how
farms feed B12 to animals and
people eat those animals. Did
you think to pray. Did you think to sing.

The night I was in the garden waiting for
the centurions to come for
me, I was praising Jesus, and He said
to me: *Are you in good hands. That's
All State's stand.*
                    Tell Mr. Reindeer
I'm going to see myself soon
in the hallway with him, the styrofoam
cherries reminding him and me: *This
moment is a monument to be built in
His memory.*

                    This memory, then, is
spectacle: the wayward
balm on your fingernail when
you júmped out the window for
that Patrick boy to come get you.
I wanted to tell on you.
Halt your peace. Change the adrenaline.
But all I did was listen to dad thrash
photo frames half the night. It was like
how you and I hated blueberries
every summer.

THE AUTOBIOGRAPHY OF FROGS

Teeth are among the most distinctive
(and long-lasting) features of the mammal species.
Humans, like other <u>frogs</u>, are diphyodont,
meaning that they develop two
<u>frogs</u> of teeth. The first set (called the
"baby," "milk," "primary," or "deciduous" _____)
normally starts to appear at about six months
of <u>frogs</u>, although some babies are born with
one or more visible teeth, known as <u>frog</u>
teeth. Normal <u>frog</u> eruption at about six
_____ is known as "teething" and can
be painful.

A GIRL WALKS HOME ALONE AT NIGHT —
FIRST KISS SCENE

3:06 – She's now completely turned around, facing Arash. She looks up, they meet eyes

> *right at "I close my eyes*

3:07 – as my hand shakes."

3:08 – She starts for the crown of his head, starts tilting his head back. We figure it out finally: she's predator, he's prey. She looks up at his throat. We watch her resisting it.

> *What's the name of the vein vampires go for.*

3:52 – She stops tilting his head back. / The music's fading. / Her cheek is pressed against his chest. He's still defenseless, on the comedown from E. / The music's still playing.

> *Is it diegetic or non-diegetic*

> *?*

> *Does it matter?*

> *It's a first kiss scene. They don't kiss.*

***

(A scene with a balloon follows. EXTERIOR – DAY – A courtyard somewhere, maybe a basketball court. Slow motion (half speed?). A trans woman is taking the balloon across the sky. She's turning, twirling. It's a dance. Is it choreographed? In Vietnamese, the word for what she's doing is *múa*. Like the rest of the movie, the scene is in black and white. So, who wouldn't assume the balloon is red.)

ZOMBIE

Her hair is radiant. Like, radiant

radiant. It has that post-illness hasn't-been-

washed glow to it.

ZOMBIES

In the next world, there's a line
of haircare products called
Convalescence:

> *Crack (Dandruff Control)*
> *Luminol (Tea Tree Oil 60% Real)*
> *Glowstick (with Yuccalyptus®)*

and cocaine is on the endangered species list.

ALCOHOLISM

pregame = blunt force trauma

blunt force trauma blunt force trauma = postgame postgame

= still functional organs after resurrection

HIGH WE ARE

Somehow we're now Harold Lloyd/Jackie Chan, letting go of the minute hand,
dropping ourselves right onto Magritte's moving steam locomotive:

If we time it just right

I bet we could get it to
catch us,

dead on the
tailbone. Right between

the washout plugs
and whistle. Zero-
backspin earth

under us, itty-bitty
clouds

all around us.

TWO ZOMBIES

Look how even now he pretends to be her little synesthete.

His truthlessness
never mattered.

They meander and bump into things;
connection's still real.

BUDDY AND BUTTERSCOTCH, WATER GOAT IN THE YEAR OF THE WATER SNAKE

After the wedding the cats

started fighting. It was our little
speedster Butterscotch. She touched
the leaves of the pale China lantern.

One way of explaining it
(I think we enjoyed debating):

I left my anger behind

while we were honeymooning;
you kept a daily vigil
alone in the mornings,

checking your inbox, beaten
by a box, putting first things first.

Imagine being surprised when discovering

that the new pope is a
short-term pope named Butterscotch.

Together we planned the details of our
trip, from the week leading up to, to the
morning of our flight back. You promised

to scoop the box more often

when we got home. I thought that was
a keen way of looking at things—me
observing you leaving here.

You vaulted from one bliss to another;
you were offering me morning vigils.

for Bobo, Ellen, Robert, and Willie

SONNET THE HEDGEHOG
after Terrance Hayes, after Tuấn Đoàn

ber when that little blue speed mouse took half
a xanny and. Remember when that lit-
tle blue speed mouse took half a xanny and.
Remember when that little blue speed mouse
took half a xanny and. Remember when
that little blue speed mouse took half a xan-
ny and. Remember when that little blue
speed mouse took half a xanny and. Remem-
ber when that little blue speed mouse took half
a xanny and. Remember when that lit-
tle blue speed mouse took half a xanny and.
Remember when that little blue speed mouse
took half a xanny and. Remember when
that little blue speed mouse took half a xan

YOUR BROTHER'S WEDDING DAY

we smile and say
No not yet

or
No, no little one

or
Maybe one day

or
We have two cats (hehe) . . .

but never
No we're unable

or
No never

or
*No she's barren, and
he's had his vasectomy already*

or
She had an abortion

or
We miscarried this morning . . .

then, if the women's faces are plump
they grow gaunt

if the men's faces are plump
they grow plumper

GIGGLING

Reminding us of
our sins against that
parish were multiple
portraits of Jesus,
hung in the
many corridors
of the monastery.

CONFESSION THERAPY

One summer, as I was cleaning out the grooves in my palm, I was living in a monastery.
One Saturday, the brothers and I hopped into two minivans to go to confession at the
nearest parish. I went in, forgot some sins, withheld some, made some up to make up
for it, then stumbled over the Act of Contrition. Later that night, I told the brothers I
had forgotten some sins; hammed it up, went back the next day, confessed the ones I
forgot, withheld some more I remembered, and then nailed the Act of Contrition. Jesus
was standing a little too close to that sheep, and we all shared a giggle about it, walking
by his portrait, in the family vans, in the cloisters with Đức Mẹ, after the Fifth Mystery.

for Thầy Nhân and Thầy Phillip

EPIGRAPH

...

*The hemlocks are the only
young thing left....*

—Anne Sexton

DETAILS

for Leslie Cheung

Which building.

What floor.

How would I get up there.
Are the elevators elegant.

Would there be other people.   Are the buttons round. Would I have to walk

past a bellhop.   Would the concierge be occupied with people

checking in and checking out.   A rooftop.   A balcony.   An

orange juice.   The room.   What's it like.

How would I get there. If I drive,
someone would have to find

my car and move it eventually. I could take a

Lyft: *Hi, I'm _____ Are you _____*

What kind of small talk then.

I could just do my routine.

It would take the least amount of energy:

Do you like Lyft better than Uber. Do you find that one is better than the other.

How long have you been working for them.

Where are you from.

Do you like this city.   Does it drive you

54

crazy.   *Do you drive much during the summer.*

                    Is it much slower then.

How long have you been driving today.   *Do you like this warm weather.*

Do you like the cold.

Am I your last passenger today.   *When did you start.*

EPITAPH

. . .

The hemlocks are the only
young thing left.

FLIGHT ATTENDANT,

To land this position, you have to be able to talk to ducks. Actual ducks. Ducks over the horizon, ducks at the end of a bottle, ducks that if they were strewn out at the edge of a pond at night and you saw them in a bit of light would trigger your phobias. Ducks on drugs. Ducks on the war on drugs. Maybe ornithophobia is really the same phobia as the one with the holes bunched all together in a sickening way: Grackles on a telephone wire are scary because they are one growing row of holes in the universe. The only person I ever knew who had feelings about the universe was someone I read about once in an interview given by his student, who said another favorite teacher of his died an agonizing, humiliating death to rectal cancer, which is to say honey oozing out of a honeycomb is sickening because nothing should be able to move that slowly. To land this position, you can't be afraid of flying, even though we may struggle when we move that fast. And how would you field the following question. Are ducks ináne?

for Catherine C

LESLIE CHEUNG IN *A CHINESE GHOST STORY*

I once heard the poet Trương Trân before reading a poem about Walt Whitman say something like, *It's one thing to be in love with Walt Whitman; it's another thing to want to fuck Walt Whitman.* I fall just short of being in love with Leslie Cheung. Like love love — the way you want someone to love love you back and you'd be happy together. Like happy happy — the way young-love emotion plus aesthete equals adventuring. Like in the first phase of *A Chinese Ghost Story*, when all the zombie things keep just barely missing out on Leslie Cheung. Like clueless cute-cute Leslie Cheung.

—

In the opening scene, it's nighttime and a lantern falls into a water bath,

then we're outside, moving along the ground. Leaves blowing.

Up six steps.

Ghosts? Zombies? Monsters?

—

In the next scene,
it's daytime. Leslie Cheung wiping his brow with his sleeve
is trying to find his way.

He's eating a chunk of bread. He bites down, and it hurts his teeth.
Slapstick Leslie is adorably hapless Leslie.

He splits a big rock with his bread. He punts the bread,
and it tears a hole in his shoe. We see his big toe.

But which direction is south?

—

Umbrellas.
No,
holes in an umbrella. Rain.

At least I haven't run into thieves.

Heavy rain. Water waterfalls down his knapsack.

—

The movie is consistent. The order of appearances of the otherworldly beings makes the arc titular:

First the zombies,

then the monster,

then the ghost,
Joey Wong, who plays
the zither.

ZOMBIE

His vomit hit the top of the lectern and then the bottom so
quickly it sounded like a trochee.

ticktock

THE JAMES MERRILL HOUSE

The ghost in the
bedroom doorway had
been trying to flirt with
me for weeks, but
I hadn't realized it yet.
If I blew by him, he'd say:
Seven seas of sadness,
which one to swim in
first. If I was bored or
restless: *Which to float on.*
When I was daydreaming
about somebody:
                    I like the
detail in the bruising.

When he finally did catch
my attention one night, his
gaze was brightening my
smile on the roof-deck, while
I beamed at my friend Inez,
who was wearing her most
awful bracelet,
                    and she lied
to me, saying I looked like a
visionary speaking into the
breeze, my hair blowing
like thàt. And I felt pretty,
and she felt pretty just
saying it.
            Then, invariably,
as things happen to you when
your suitor is another species,
or is a specter, or you

have nothing but derisive
things to say about him,

he evened us out when
he said to me:

My shadow
falling across you

makes it look like
you're wearing a toga.

If we didn't have to
realize then, with such finality,
that we couldn't curb him
forever, or put him on ice,
or silence him; whether
Inez and I could have sustained
our spark, dazzling in our
friendship, helping ourselves
to curiosity during a time when
we were so optimally realized, as
we lied to each other kindly and
absolutely, we'll never know.

OXYTOCIN — A RABBIT, A HORSE

They put liquor in
the batter. I've
never seen anything like it...

If he says he'd had, he'd be lying, and she'd know it

but would pretend
all the same to
be in awe of his worldliness

and think nŏthing of performing the service.

Just a few weeks ago she tricked little Noah,

when he asked her if
they were walking on the same
street as the ice cream store, and she said *No, it's in another town that's*

not far away, looks
much like this one indeed,
and *what a smart boy you are.* Just like his

father. You'd be able to see him, in his swift rosy pride,

lost that he had
wanted ice cream in the
first place. If you asked him

about it then, he no longer needed any.

ELECTROCONVULSIVE THERAPY (ECT)
for Catherine H

It seemed like your dream within a dream made you feel like

you were being watched.

                                    Was it the meat sitting on the

opposite couch, with its forgiveness eye—backlit, and the vitreous

opaque and tonic-like—

                         who, considering thoughtfully whether

to wake you, touched its one clear mole, making it impossible for

us to settle on one story

                              or on any anecdote at all

that could help explain the scabbing over the cupboard,
                                           which

up to that point had healed whatever our joy had diminished.

If it's helpful,

                     next time I can dropkick this pen into your dream,

and you'll wake up with it on your couch. And when you wake

up, you'll wake up holding it in bed.

TTY'ALLL ETC.

Like when your dog

died and his fleas took on the
ambition of rodents

and jumped ship.

Straight into the
ocean—

giant patch of clovers

behind the locked
barrel.

ZOMBIES

emaciating cat staring out the window

[wind chimes jingling]

HI, QUASIMODO (INCHING OUT OF A DARK PLACE IN WHICH HE IS VERY SAD AND _____ WANTS TO NOT BE HERE)

You're not finished collecting
data on this side yet.
Everything here has been tested

and to be trusted, and so many
honest people came
before you—

same intentions,
same feel for what's sweet
and what's bittersweet.

It's unlike Jacques Tourneur's
Cat People principle: What
are people most afraid of?

In the dark, you don't
have to show the monster;
you leave it up to

the imagination of
the audience. Like
how director Douglas Sirk

said he always trusted
his audience to have
imagination (or else

they should stay out of
the theater).
And then there's

the side of the dark you're in,
which is expansive
and where your pace is slow

because you can't
see more than a couple feet
ahead of you. Then at some

point in the movie, you're
the monster and you discover
the movie's next victim, who is

also a monster—
but in human form.
It's true, you realize then,

that the best thing
for the group is having y'all's
own personal bad guy die first.

Why not leave the gibbet soon—
turn everyone into
your little song lemmings.

ENDORPHINS

He asks Esmeralda about her new tattoo
It's a star.

He asks what's the meaning behind it
It's a star I'm a star.

Last night she was wearing embellished cat-eye glasses, and he wanted her to know
he knew those words

Now he can't really bring it up because maybe the tattoo was already there the
whole time under the lens—dark enough from

far away to hide her cheek, glaringly

clear now that he could see the
new ink

     Did it hùrt

MECHANICAL PENCIL

for Amy

Do you capitalize phobias? Do you capitalize job titles when they're attached to people. You capitalize the shorthand of a degree but not the degree spelled out. At my job we leave out the Oxford comma, which sometimes gets us into trouble when it comes to clarity and always gets us into trouble when we leave the comma in there and forget to take it out, and our boss strikes through it. How do you spell the phobia with the gross holes. I've never Googled it because I don't want to risk seeing images. A friend once warned me never to do so. I've tried every variation I can think of, in Microsoft Word, but they all come up wrong. Maybe Word doesn't know that phobia. Or maybe it has that fear, too. Every variation I try has that line under it: red, squiggly, foreboding failure. Having a fear of birds is called ornithophobia. I know this because I Googled it. Also, Gmail used to not know how to spell its own name lol

NOSFERATU: A SYMPHONY OF HORROR —
FIRST GOODBYE SCENE
(INTERTITLES REMIX)

and away

more glowing
finally

-

the rich ship-owner
his wife
his sister

many became the ghosts the Karpathen could see to

-

the country
the dusty roads worried the
horses

-

thieves travelled
far for it

-

do not worry, Harding, I'm going with friends of
of

-

but
he

Hutter and his
his

-

left it difficult to travel young

LAST BREATH BEFORE SHEEP

You want to remember what he smells like, but you also
want to remember something new.

What can we call the last sheep you count. Or the breath
you take as you cross over into sleep.

The way meat still smells good to you—vegan you—
"The Star-Spangled Banner" still gives you the chills. You want to live

in a world where Starmie evolves into Staryu, not the other way around.
It's not impossible to find someone who can put you first, Bright Star.

When people have a baby, their baby looks like them.
And then they become unmistakable for their baby.

14

for L.

Three minutes and seven seconds. Remember our list of cats?

      Two were days of the week, a dozen the names of flowers
we took from a calendar. One year for your birthday

you saw a rabbit on the lawn and made a wish with an eyelash.

Yesterday, grazing on the same aster, a humble bee and
a bumblebee. You pierced my ear with a safety pin, we attached

and pushed off. April: a butterfly paused center frame,

white pushpin above the lavender haze of its wing. March: Istanbul with
birds and bonnets.

      The kinds of gifts I give, you can find in

a curio store.
      I like to think I provide the context exceptionally

well, though: documenting every little serendipitous thing with

narratives voiced over images of landmarks.
Didn't we say we preferred this kind of courtship. I charge you

for all the memories you've forgotten that I remember.
My rate is much higher than yours,

                    even though you have
memories, too. There's a flower called strawberry fields.

I'm telling you. There's a flower called sixteen candles.

I have a Bird in spring
Which for myself doth sing—
The spring decoys.
And as the summer nears—
And as the Rose appears,
Robin is gone.

Yet do I not repine
Knowing that Bird of mine
Though flown—
Learneth beyond the sea
Melody new for me
And will _____.

—Emily Dickinson

MAD LIB WITH _____ IN IT

Most eye floaters are

caused by age-related

<u>river</u> that occurs as

the <u>whiskey</u>-like substance

(vitreous) inside your eyes

becomes more liquid.

<u>30,000</u> microscopic <u>dissolved</u>

<u>tablets</u> within the <u>big big</u>

<u>water</u> tend to clump

and can cast tiny shadows

on your retina. The <u>hoodie</u> _____

<u>be wearing</u> is called a floater.

BREVITY

In his note, Leslie Cheung mentioned depression and how he couldn't stand it anymore. He said it was a tough year. He thanked his friends, his psychiatrist, his family, two others. And then he asks a question.

LESLIE CHEUNG IN *A CHINESE GHOST STORY*

We're dry again, in the daylight. There's music around us, small, thin paper slips blowing around.

A festival? Which one?

—

The noise of people all around.

It's hard not to read real life tragedy into this
film and see his death in every scene.

—

Someone in the dispersing crowd yells out to him,

You! You've money for the dead stuck on you! Trying to take advantage of me?

Sir, you've got to be joking! I don't spend this kind of money.

(*You'll be able to spend it sooner or later.*)

—

He tells the people he has free lodging at the haunted temple, Lan Yeuk.

How brave

He's going to die

Let him go

We shouldn't let him go

—

It's night again. Three wolves, eyes glowing green.

Leslie Cheung, cutely: *Hey don't eat me! If you eat me, then I'll be dead.*

—

cute
cute
tragic
cute
cute
tragicute

cute

cute
tragic
cute

I think that's the ratio for this movie

—

so that she, Joey Wong, the beautiful woman in the painting, his love interest, the ghost, can be mortal again . . .

—

The first time they meet: Ivory White Transparent Curtains No Liner No Grommets Non-Textured Linen Curtains for Wooden Pier, 2 Panels,

flowing in the breeze.

—

While he's unconscious under her spell, she says to him,
You seem rather kind. It's a shame you came to the wrong place,
or else you wouldn't have to die such a wrongful death.

—

Her burial urn,
black, calabash gourd-shaped,
needs to be reburied somewhere safe.

—

Or else I won't make it in time to reincarnate as a mortal.

—

    The scene where we know they know they're in love,
    they're writing a love poem together on a scroll.
    They take turns writing lines.

"Envious of mandarin ducks   eternal love rather than, the immortality of the gods."

HART <3

1929, 1935, 1974, 1963, 1964, 1938, 1969, 1912, 1984, 1972, 1951, 1982, 2009, 1950, 1996, 1978, 1941, 1857, 1984, 1996, 1956, 1937, 2003, 1941, 1921, 1970, 65 CE, 2002, 1926, 1974, 278 BCE, 1978, 2007, 1928, 1933, c. 684 or 686, 1990, 1970, 1945, 2003, 1923, 1929, 1919, 1947, 1945, _____ , 1770, 1966, 1925, 2009, 1991, 1976, 1914, 1998, 1367, 1974.

> *. . . Don't read this just as death wish;*
> *Crane was unusually full of life.*

—Robert Lowell/Elise Partridge

ZOMBIES

emaciating cat staring out the window

[wind chimes jingling]

SEROTONIN — THE THIRTIETH WEEK OF THE YEAR OF THE EARTH PIG

We both crush on tragedy, your vantage point
giving you the upper hand, and áfter some time
I will disappear into the corners of the room;

the thought of this sacrifice fills me with tenderness,
no matter the outcome. When you say things like

smell your foot to see if it's rotting, I know I
can't get this from anyone else. There was that night
we gave up on the meteors and started counting

fireflies, the way some couples keep trying for
monotony, like when the neighborhood squirrels
died and the acorns stayed buried.

If we skip matrimony, we need to skip last rites too—
both direct objects have to obey the same predicate.
The earth is moving fast, but these clouds are moving

faster. Same questions: Wháts ur birthday.

                                                 R ů ticklish

YEAR OF THE DOGS, YEAR OF A SYNAPSE

for asl

            Which is why I point out
you helped make me cross a scary bridge. It
probably never occurred to you that
the planks were very far apart.

And I hadn't thought about water.
Then we had to go into work right
after and put in a long honest shift.
Life is colorless when I'm not crying. I
forget you knew that about me so quickly.

TWO SCENES FROM *I WALKED WITH A ZOMBIE*

Previous caretaker:
It's just like dressing a great big doll.

(about Mrs. Holland, the Zombie)

—

Man 6:
She doesn't bleed!

Woman 4:
Z_____!

Man 6:
She doesn't bleed!

(about Mrs. Holland again)

"WONG KAR-WAI CAT"

noun

Every moment it's a beautified pose, this cat.

Pause any Wong Kar-wai film

at any one moment and

you have *Casablanca*.

Except sometimes when the cat is sleeping.

And except when the cat's humans are gone.

for Cathy

NOREPINEPHRINE — SUICIDES IN FICTION SAY GOODBYE

I don't mean this room, Frank.
I mean this world.
   (American Horror Story 2:7)

Give 11 dollars to the next person who asks.
And then 7, or 10, or 9: all of your siblings'
jersey numbers until you honor them all. . .
Adam kicks a votive candle clean off the stoop
and wishes he could obliterate the candle before
he completes his follow-through. He resents
the street because it can. Thu Vân sells her
owl collection, in one go—leaves not one
behind. Jinny keeps her best shoes, buys
new laces, and relaces them. She learns the
lattice method. Dee starts signing their emails
different, turning every "Best," into "<3,"
turning every "<3," into "Love,." Quasimodo
stops being pretentious. Daisy stops caring
when she stutters. She stops that stupid
postmortem-loop-for-days-after. Miles
masters the double-under and then teaches
someone how to start learning it. Violet
lets someone teach her the two-step. Lux
abstains from being charismatic for three
days and then apologizes to all their loved
ones for at least one thing. For Mike, it's
listen to Getter/Joji, dream about moving
to Los Angeles, listen to "Angeles." For Anna,
it's listen to *Anna Karenina* on tape. Leo
bounces up and down, dances all night,
writes all morning, sleeps an hour. Cecilia
loves big, still—and refuses to stop. Neil
sees an onion ring in a shopping cart and

remembers eating a giant plate late one
night with a friend. He gets two large
orders from Sonic and feeds them to his
dog all day. Damien prays that God will
bless his neighbors and his devils. Jason
touches thirteen mailboxes. Lane rewatches
the Subway Series on VHS. He makes Cracker
Jacks from popcorn with butter and sugar.
Jen Yu pours herself a celebratory drink and
makes everyone think it's a courage drink.
Jesus lets earth into his mouth to give thanks.

NOREPINEPHRINE — THREE METHODS

-

Whispering underwater

        with Virginia Woolf:

There was a door shutting
        every hour we woke.

-

Splitting 9
small
    atoms with Grumpy Cat.

-

Under the next
    Blue Line train

        to Wonderland.

ZOMBIE

ZOMBIE

ZOMBIE

ZOMBIE

Maybe then she remembers
                              briefly

she once saw the northern lights.

NOTES

DIACRITICS:

Zombie Vomit Mad Libs combines English words with Vietnamese diacritics. Vietnamese diacritical marks instruct a reader on how to pronounce a word, by indicating which tone to use, or more specifically, which pitch to use when saying vowels. Written English, in most cases, does not provide complete information on how to say a word using the appropriate pitch for a given context. Written Vietnamese, because Vietnamese is a tonal language, gives a reader closer to complete information regarding pronunciation.

For written English, there's only one instance I can think of in which the pitch (not emphasis) is clearly indicated, and that's the question mark. For example, "What are you doing?" The question mark tells us to read the final vowel sound with a rising pitch. In Vietnamese, that pitch is indicated by the diacritic *sắc*. (For the vowel *a*, the symbol *sắc* yields *á*.)

Grammatical rules aside, consider the same sentence punctuated by a period: "What are you doing." This is one possible way to eliminate the rising pitch. What's left instead is a sentence that ends with either a falling pitch or a pitch that neither rises nor falls.

Here's the same question with different punctuation:

(a) "What are you doing?"
This sentence could indicate a social context in which the speaker doesn't know what the other person is doing and the speaker genuinely wants to know.

(b) "What are you doing."
This sentence could indicate a social context in which the speaker does in fact know what the other person is doing and the speaker is frustrated. A falling pitch or a neutral pitch at the end of this sentence might tell us that the speaker thinks the other person has bad judgement or is doing something wrong.

These two sentences demonstrate the only ways I can think of to indicate pitch in written English. In the case of *Zombie Vomit Mad Libs*, combining English words with Vietnamese diacritics can maybe tell us a little bit more about _____ (about zombies maybe).

CONTAGION
Leonardo da Vinci's portrait painting, *Lady with an Ermine* (*Dama con l'ermellino*) (1489–1491).

Johannes Vermeer's portrait painting, *Girl with a Pearl Earring* (*Meisje met de parel*) (c. 1665).

FLEAS,
In 1973, the United States military began its exit campaign from Vietnam.

iPhone VC
"VC": Việt Cộng, political party in South Vietnam and Cambodia whose military forces fought against the United States and South Vietnamese governments in the Vietnam War.

"worth shooting at," 'rotated back': from the 1987 war drama film *Full Metal Jacket*, directed by Stanley Kubrick.

POET SUICIDES, THIRTEEN-PENTAMETER SONNET
Humberto Fierro
René Crevel
Sophie Podolski
Sylvia Plath
Michel Bernanos
Antonia Pozzi
José María Arguedas
Arturo Borja
Richard Brautigan
John Berryman
Konstantin Biebl
Jane Arden
Rachel Wetzsteon
John Gould Fletcher
Amelia Rosselli
Danielle Collobert

Karin Boye
Dolores Veintimilla
Sara Shagufta
May Ayim
Jan Lechoń
Jean-Joseph Rabearivelo
Yun Hyon-seok
Marina Tsvetaeva
Teresa Wilms Montt
Yukio Mishima
Lucan
Allen Upward
Jaime Torres Bodet
Qu Yuan
Eli Siegel
Liam Rector
Charlotte Mew
Sara Teasdale
Lu Zhaolin
Joe Bolton
Paul Celan
Pierre Eugène Drieu La Rochelle
María Mercedes Carranza
Jacques Rigaut
Anna Wickham
Arthur Davison Ficke
Hart Crane
Thomas Chatterton
Chen Mengjia
Sergei Yesenin
Yulia Drunina
Jens Bjørneboe
Rozz Williams
Zhao Luanluan
Anne Sexton

MAD LIB WITH ANNE SEXTON

Text adapted from mayoclinic.org page about eye floaters.

On October 4, 1974, Anne Sexton died of carbon monoxide poisoning in the garage of her home in Weston, Massachusetts. Before she died, she took off her rings, put on her mother's fur coat, and poured herself a glass of vodka.

2046 IS ON THE 24TH FLOOR
"It's just that he goes around hurting a lot of Tonies": adapted from angie sijun lou.

On April 1, 2003, Leslie Cheung died after jumping from his 24th-floor hotel room at the Mandarin Oriental, Hong Kong.

ZOMBIE BABIES
"one baby to another": from the 1991 Nirvana song, "Drain You," written by Kurt Cobain.

LET THE RIGHT ONE IN – FIRST MEETING SCENE (IN REWIND)
Let the Right One In (Swedish: *Låt den rätte komma in*): 2008 romantic horror film, directed by Tomas Alfredson; starring Kåre Hedebrant, Lina Leandersson, and Per Ragnar; based on the 2004 novel of the same title by John Ajvide Lindqvist.

"TALE OF THE TAPE"
"Tale of the Tape" is an expression in combat sports, such as boxing and mixed martial arts, which refers to a set of prefight comparisons between two opponents: age, height, weight, reach, fight record, number of KOs, TKOs, or submissions.

A GIRL WALKS HOME ALONE AT NIGHT – FIRST KISS SCENE
A Girl Walks Home Alone at Night: 2014 horror Western Persian-language film, directed by Ana Lily Amirpour, starring Sheila Vand and Arash Marandi.

ZOMBIES AT A CROSS SIGNAL
Lines adapted from "Mr. Mine," from *Love Poems* (Houghton Mifflin Company, 1967) by Anne Sexton.

THE AUTOBIOGRAPHY OF FROGS
Text adapted from the Wikipedia entry: Tooth.

HIGH WE ARE
Harold Lloyd in the 1923 silent romantic-comedy film *Safety Last!*, directed by Sam Taylor and Fred C. Newmeyer.

Jackie Chan in the 1983 martial arts action-comedy film *Project A*, directed by Jackie Chan.

"moving steam locomotive": from René Magritte's 1938 painting *Time Transfixed (La Durée poignardée)*.

SONNET THE HEDGEHOG
After "Sonnet" (about watermelons) by Terrance Hayes. Title by *Tuấn Đoàn*.

CONFESSION THERAPY
"Đức Mẹ": Mother Mary (Maria).

EPIGRAPH
Adapted from "Eighteen Days Without You," from *Love Poems* (Houghton Mifflin Company, 1967) by Anne Sexton.

LESLIE CHEUNG IN *A CHINESE GHOST STORY*
A Chinese Ghost Story: 1987 romantic comedy horror film, directed by Ching Siu-tung, starring Leslie Cheung and Joey Wong.

THE JAMES MERRILL HOUSE
The James Merrill House: "A National Historic Landmark in Stonington, Connecticut, the 1901 James Merrill House is a late-Victorian commercial & residential building significant for its forty-one-year association with American poet James Ingram Merrill" (https://jamesmerrillhouse.org, June 1, 2024).

HI, QUASIMODO (INCHING OUT OF A DARK PLACE IN WHICH HE IS VERY SAD AND _____ WANTS TO NOT BE HERE)
Cat People: 1942 horror film, directed by Jacques Tourneur, starring Simone Simon.

ENDORPHINS
"It's a star," "It's a star I'm a star": adapted from UFC fighter Sean O'Malley.

NOSFERATU: A SYMPHONY OF HORROR – FIRST GOODBYE SCENE (INTERTITLES REMIX)
Text adapted from four intertitles in the first goodbye scene of *Nosferatu: A Symphony of Horror* (German: *Nosferatu – Eine Symphonie des Grauens*), 1922 silent film directed by F.W. Murnau, starring Max Schreck.

LAST BREATH BEFORE SHEEP

Starmie: "Starmie is a dual-type Water/Psychic Pokémon introduced in Generation I. It evolves from Staryu when exposed to a Water Stone" (bulbapedia.bulbagarden.net).

Staryu: "Staryu is a Water-type Pokémon introduced in Generation I. It evolves into Starmie when exposed to a Water Stone" (bulbapedia.bulbagarden.net).

"Bright Star": from John Keats' poem, "Bright star, would I were stedfast as thou art."

HART <3

On April 27, 1932, Hart Crane leapt from the steamship Orizaba into the Gulf of Mexico. His body was never recovered.

". . . Don't read this just as death wish; / Crane was unusually full of life": from Elise Partridge's poem, "Four Lectures by Robert Lowell" (section I "'On Repose of Rivers' by Hart Crane"), from *Chameleon Hours* (University of Chicago Press, 2008).

Partridge was a student of Lowell's. In the poem, she recalls his teachings on Crane.

TWO SCENES FROM *I WALKED WITH A ZOMBIE*

I Walked with a Zombie: 1943 horror film directed by Jacques Tourneur; starring Frances Dee, Tom Conway, James Ellison, and Christine Gordon.

NOREPINEPHRINE – SUICIDES IN FICTION SAY GOODBYE

Epigraph (Miles speaking to Frank McCann) taken from *American Horror Story* season 2, episode 7, "Dark Cousin," directed by Michael Rymer and written by Tim Minear (2012).

NOREPINEPHRINE – THREE METHODS

On March 28th, 1941, Virginia Woolf died by drowning, in the River Ouse.

"There was a door shutting / every hour we woke.": adapted from Virginia Woolf's short story, "A Haunted House," from her collection *Monday or Tuesday* (1921).

Wonderland: Greater Boston's Blue Line train's final stop.

ACKNOWLEDGMENTS

Grateful acknowledgment to the following publications in which these poems first appeared, sometimes in slightly different versions:

The American Poetry Review – "Poet Suicides, Thirteen-Pentameter Sonnet,"
   "Brevity," "Details," "Mad Lib with Anne Sexton," "Mad Lib with ___ in It"
The Baffler – "Flight Attendant,"
Columbia Journal – "Endorphins," "Oxytocin — A Rabbit, a Horse"
Columbia Journal Online – "A Little Bit Dopamine, a Little Bit Conversation"
The Common – "Norepinephrine — Suicides in Fiction Say Goodbye"
Denver Quarterly – "Everything Means Nothing Compares"
Four Way Review – "Mechanical Pencil"
The Georgia Review – "Dopamine," "Last Breath Before Sheep," "Serotonin —
   The Thirtieth Week of the Year of the Earth Pig," "Year of the Dogs, Year of
   a Synapse"
Kenyon Review – "Buddy and Butterscotch, Water Goat in the Year of the Water
   Snake," "Oxytocin," "Oxytocin — Siblings"
The Margins – "2046 is on the 24th Floor"
The North American Review – "The James Merrill House"
The Offing – "Leslie Cheung in *A Chinese Ghost Story*," "Leslie Cheung in *A
   Chinese Ghost Story*"
Plume – "Confession Therapy," "Electroconvulsive Therapy (ECT)"
Poetry Northwest – "14," "Your Brother's Wedding Day"
Poetry Online – "Hi, Quasimodo (inching out of a dark place in which he is very
   sad and _____ wants to not be here)"
Strange Horizons – "High We Are"

Special thanks to Robert Hildreth for his generosity through Boston University's Robert Pinsky Global Fellowship.

Forever love and gratitude to Bridge, Emily, Nghiệp, MâyMây, and Mèo. And for their support of the book and/or care after the fire, to Anh Dao, Brian, Cathy, Cesar, Cô Loan, Ivy, Jade, Jae, Jessie, Naomi, Judson, Laura, Louise, Phương, Rana, Robert, Sammy, Sara, Sara, Sarah, Tamiko, Tomas, Trenton, and Wo.

RECENT TITLES FROM ALICE JAMES BOOKS

ALICE JAMES BOOKS is committed to publishing books that matter. The press was founded in 1973 in Boston, Massachusetts to give women access to publishing. As a cooperative, authors performed the day-to-day undertakings of the press. The press continues to expand and grow from its formative roots, guided by its founding values of access, excellence, inclusivity, and collaboration in publishing. Its mission is to publish books that matter and preserve a place of belonging for poets who inspire us. AJB seeks to broaden our collective interpretation of what constitutes the American poetic voice and is dedicated to helping its artists achieve purposeful engagement with broad audiences and communities nationwide. The press was named for Alice James, sister to William and Henry, whose extraordinary gift for writing went unrecognized during her lifetime.

Designed by Alban Fischer
Printed by Versa Press